Roy of the Rovers

"EASTERN PROMISE"

D1439514

RAVETTE BOOKS

Printed and bound for Ravette Books Limited,
3 Glenside Estate, Star Road,
Partridge Green, Horsham,
West Sussex RH13 8RA.
An Egmont Company
by Proost International Bookproduction, Belgium.
ISBN: 1 85304 179 3

17-YEAR-OLD GARY GUNN HAD BEEN INCLUDED IN THE YOUTH SQUAD...

YOU MIGHT EVEN DISCOVER A *NEW STAR*, ROY...LIKE *ME* !

OR AN APPETITE FOR RAW FISH ! SHUT UP AND SIT DOWN, GARY !

CHEER UP, BOSS...IT COULD BE A LAUGH ! I MEAN, YOU CAN COUNT ON THE JAPANESE TO DO THINGS IN STYLE !

TERRY SPRING WAS RIGHT !

...A MARCHING BAND... GUARD OF HONOUR ! HORDES OF OFFICIALS !

AND THIS IS JUST FOR THE *YOUTH TEAM*..!

GREETINGS, ROY RACE SAN ! WE HEARD THAT YOU HAD MADE A LAST-MINUTE DECISION TO VISIT US !

I AM *ICHIO TANAKA* — ORGANISER OF THE TOUR, AND OUR PRESTIGIOUS TOURNAMENT !

ER, **WHAT** TOURNAMENT ?

ALL WILL BE EXPLAINED ! IN MEANTIME, WE HAVE ARRANGED SPECIAL WELCOME FOR ILLUSTRIOUS ROVERS ! PLEASE TO FOLLOW US INTO THE HANGAR...!

HE IS COMING ! ACTIVATE *COHERENT RADIATION UNIT* !

...ROY RACE ! HE BEATS **ONE** MAN — **TWO** MEN..!

HUUUUH ?

WHAT THE..?

A GIANT *HOLOGRAM* OF ROY — AN IMAGE CAST BY *COHERENT LIGHT RADIATION!*

OR TO PUT IT MORE **SIMPLY** — AN ELECTRONIC *GIMMICK...!*

YES, MR. TANAKA, IT'S JUST AN **IMAGE** OF ME! IT'S TIME YOUR PEOPLE WERE TREATED TO THE *REAL THING...!*

UUUH?

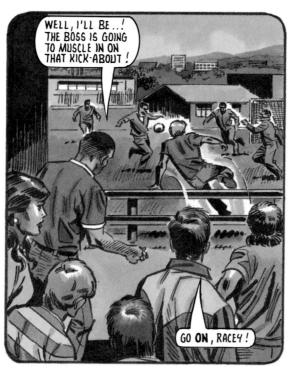

WELL, I'LL BE...! THE BOSS IS GOING TO MUSCLE IN ON THAT KICK-ABOUT!

GO **ON**, RACEY!

NEVER TAKE YOUR EYE OFF THE BALL, SON...!

HAI!

SOON...

YOU DON'T SEEM SO UPSET AT MISSING OUT ON YOUR HOLIDAY, ROY !

I WAS AT FIRST, SPRINGO... BUT OUR HOSTS HAVE GOT ME GOING A BIT ! THIS WHOLE TOUR IS TURNING OUT TO BE A BIT OF A CHALLENGE..!

APART FROM THAT, I DON'T GET AS MUCH CHANCE TO WORK WITH YOU LADS AS I WOULD LIKE...NOT AT HOME, ANYWAY ! SO SPLIT UP INTO TWO SQUADS....!

...YOU'RE GOING TO LEARN SOME MELCHESTER MAGIC !

YEAH ! LET'S GIVE 'EM THE BUSINESS, ROY ...I MEAN, BOSS !

COME ON ... WHERE'S THE SUPPORT ? IT'S NO USE PASSING THE BALL AND THEN DROPPING OUT OF THE GAME !

LET YOUR TEAM-MATES KNOW WHERE YOU ARE..!

ROY'S SON, LITTLE RACEY, WAS PLAYING IN ONE OF THE GOALS...

HELLO ! WHAT'S THAT BLOKE UP TO....?

THERE'S ANOTHER ONE OVER THERE ! I...I THINK HE'S SPYING ON US....!

...I RECKON THEY'RE GOING TO COPY OUR STYLE AND TACTICS !

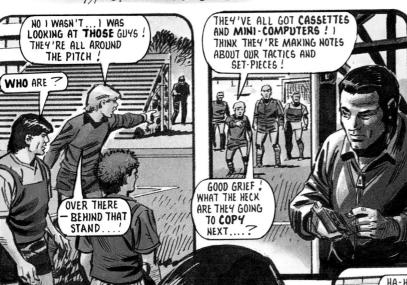

AA-AAAACH!

WE COULD MAKE THE MISTAKE OF TAKING IT ALL TOO EASILY...LIKE GARY GUNN!

HE'S **LOST** IT..!

IT WAS THE SIGNAL FOR AN EXCITED OUTBURST ON THE PART OF THE KOREAN COACH...

WHAT THE HECK'S ALL **THAT** ABOUT..?

...THEY WERE SETTING US UP FOR THE KOREANS!

THE KOREANS ARE FORMING THEMSELVES INTO A LITTLE **PACK** — LIKE **WE** DO!

WELL, I'LL BE...! THAT'S **MELCHESTER POSSESSION** STUFF..!

NOW WE KNOW WHAT TANAKA'S **SPIES** WERE DOING..!

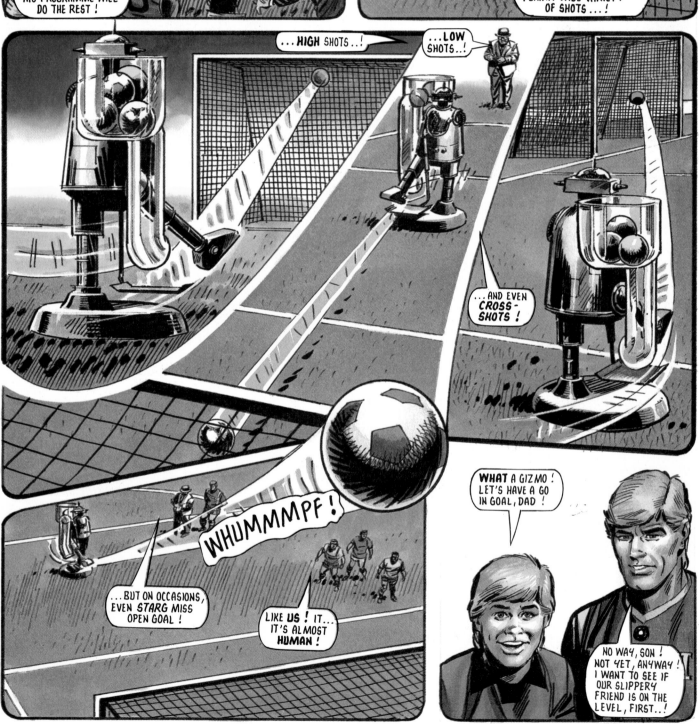

...THAT BALL MUST HAVE BEEN TRAVELLING LIKE A BULLET! HE'S STILL *CONCUSSED*!

POOR KID! LET'S HOPE IT HAS CLEARED UP BY TOMORROW...!

BUT, THE FOLLOWING DAY...

...I'M AFRAID THERE HAS BEEN LITTLE IMPROVEMENT IN NICKY WATSON'S CONDITION, GENTLEMEN!

AND YOU'RE PLAYING THE AMERICANS THIS EVENING, ROY! WHO WILL BE TAKING HIS PLACE IN GOAL?

ME! TO MY GREAT SURPRISE, THE ORGANISING COMMITTEE RAISED NO OBJECTION!

I'M NOT SURPRISED! ONCE IT GETS ROUND THAT ROY RACE IS PLAYING, THE PUNTERS WILL COME *FLOCKING* IN!

LITTLE RACEY!

HA! HA! HA!

IT WAS THE ROVERS' TURN TO PLAY 'OUT OF TOWN'...

THE JAPS ARE PLAYING KOREA IN THE CHAMPIONSHIP STADIUM...SO WE'RE AT HAMPDEN!

GOOD GRIEF! DON'T TELL ME THEY'VE BUILT A REPLICA OF *HAMPDEN PARK*, AS WELL AS WEMBLEY!

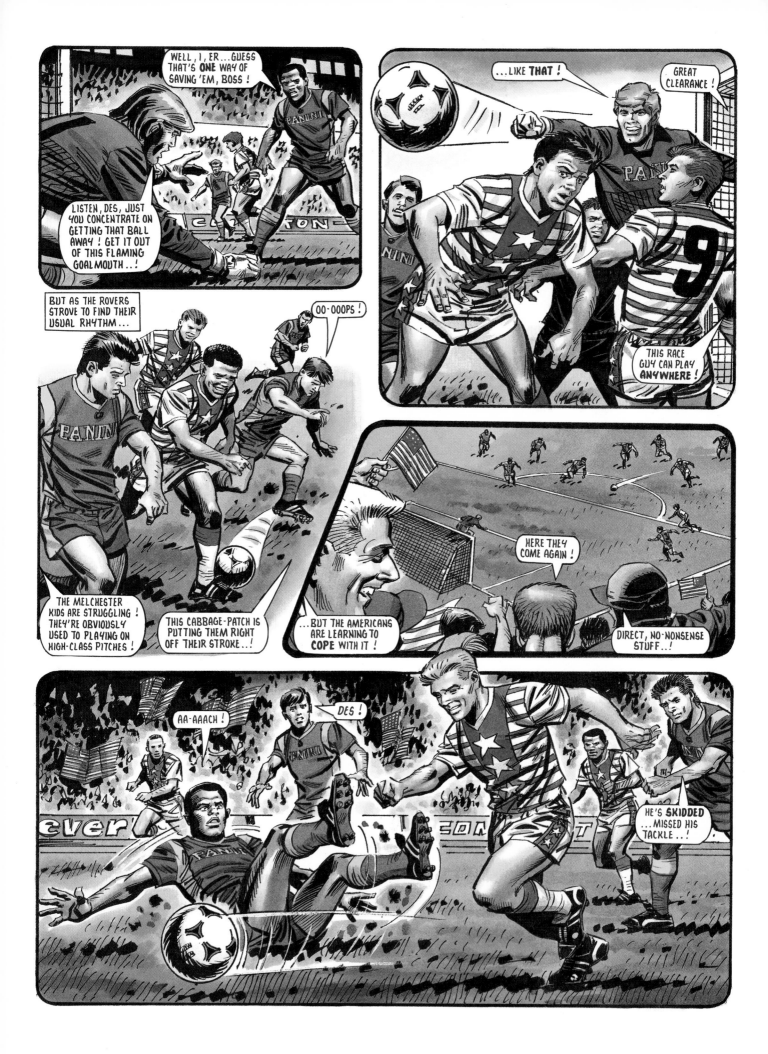

...LONG BALL STUFF ?...AGAIN ?

I KNOW — IT BREAKS MY HEART, TOO ! YOU DON'T NEED A REF FOR THAT KIND OF FOOTBALL...YOU NEED AN AIR-TRAFFIC CONTROLLER..!

BUT IT'S THE ONLY WAY ON THIS SURFACE ! CUT OUT THE FRILLS, AND START KNOCKING IT AROUND !

GIVE THE BALL PLENTY OF AIR...!

...AND THAT MEANS YOU, TOO, GARY GUNN !

NO WAY ! I'M KEEPING THE BALL ON THE DECK...!

HEY—!

...I DON'T NEED KICK-AND-STUFF TO SORT OUT THESE YANKS...!

THIS GUY'S TRICKY ! LOOK AT HIM GO...!

YEEAAAAH !

...AN' NOW YOU'RE GONE, GARY... THANKS TO THE PITCH !

YOU HEARD WHAT THE BOSS SAID...!

...LONG BALLS, AN' NO MESSIN'!

IT'S YOURS, TOMMY JOHNSON...!

LOOK AT *ROY RACE*, COACH! SEEMS LIKE HE'S COMING UP TO TAKE THE PENALTY!

HE CAN'T DO *THAT*! HE GOT SPECIAL PERMISSION TO PLAY IN GOAL, BUT THAT'S AS FAR AS IT GOES!

HEY, RACE...ARE YOUR PLAYERS SUCH NAMBY-PAMBIES THAT YOU EVEN GOTTA TAKE THE *PENALTIES* FOR 'EM?

NO...!

YOU SEEM TO FORGET THAT I HAPPEN TO BE THEIR *MANAGER*! I CAN'T VERY WELL GIVE THEM MY ADVICE IF I'M STUCK BACK IN MY GOAL, CAN I....?

AT LEAST I HAVEN'T GOT SOMEONE IN THE CROWD GIVING ME ADVICE THROUGH TOY EAR-PHONES! OR MAYBE YOU'RE LISTENING TO THE TOP TEN?

I-I... WHADDYA SAY?

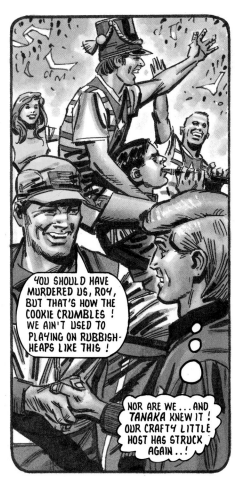

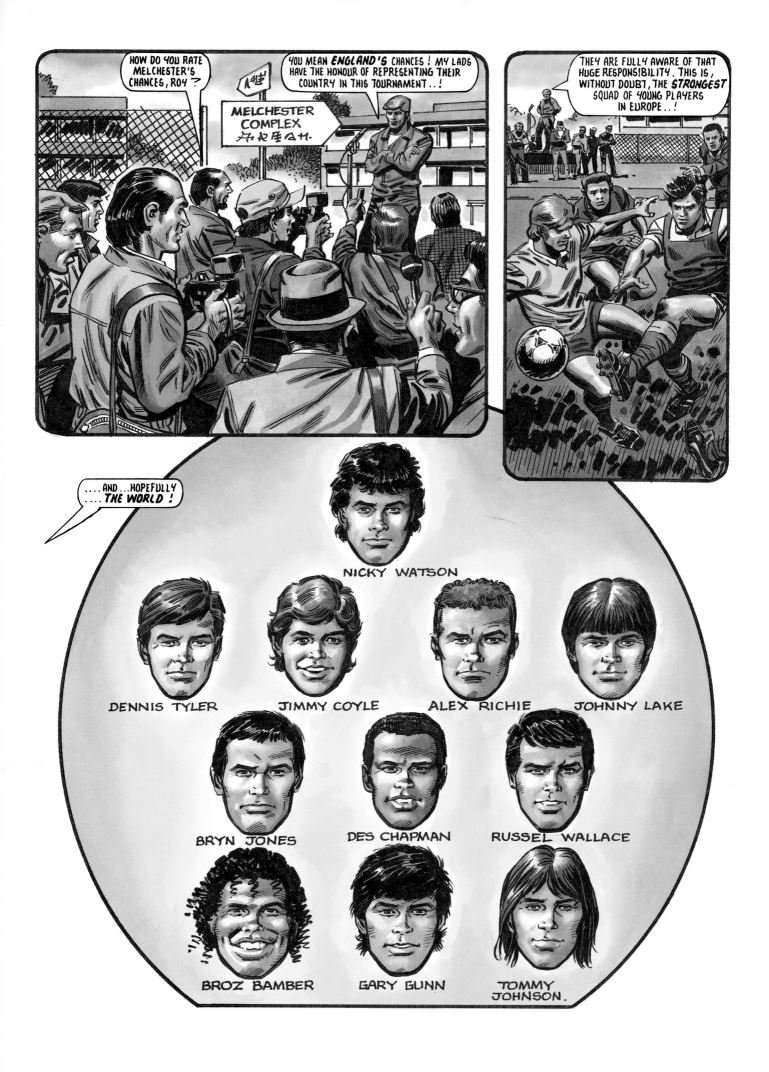

AS THE PRESS CONFERENCE BROKE UP...

HEY, BOSS! TAKE A LOOK OVER THERE... THE MAIN STADIUM!

JAPAN'S VERSION OF *WEMBLEY*! WHAT ABOUT IT, JIMMY COYLE?

THEY'RE CARRYING OUT SOME LAST-MINUTE MAINTENANCE WORK... BUT LOOK WHO'S UP ON THE PLATFORM...!

IT'S *TANAKA*! HE'S *STILL* SPYING ON US..!

SO WHAT? HE'S HIT US WITH EVERY LITTLE DODGE HE COULD THINK OF...!

...ROBOT STRIKERS, DODGY PITCHES! AND WE'VE SURVIVED IT ALL — APART FROM THAT HICCUP AGAINST THE UNITED STATES!

FAMOUS LAST WORDS!

HAAAIIIIII!

JAAAAA-PAN!

THERE ISN'T A SINGLE TRICK HE'S GOT LEFT UP HIS SLEEVE!

I DON'T *BELIEVE* THIS! TANAKA'S DONE IT AGAIN..!

JAAAAA-PAN!

ROVERS!

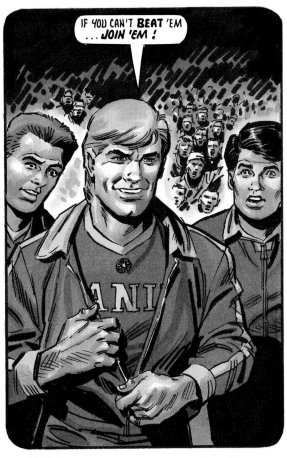

IF YOU CAN'T **BEAT** 'EM ...**JOIN** 'EM !

AIEEEEEEE ! LOOK ! ROY RACE COMES ON AS SUBSTITUTE !

GREATEST PLAYER IN WORLD SETS HIMSELF AGAINST **MERE YOUTHS** !

BOOOOOOOO !

YOU ARE JOKING, OF COURSE ! THIS TOURNAMENT IS RESTRICTED TO PLAYERS UNDER THE AGE OF EIGHTEEN !

WHO SAYS **I'M** NOT UNDER EIGHTEEN, REF..?

YOU SHOW ME **THEIR** BIRTH-CERTIFICATES... **AND** I'LL SHOW YOU MINE !

TO THE AMAZEMENT AND DISMAY OF THE MELCHESTER PLAYERS...

HE'S SHAMED THE REF INTO ALLOWING HIM TO STAY ON ! BUT HE...HE **CAN'T** !

IT'S **RIGHT** OVER THE TOP !

ROY RACE HAS JUST MADE US LOOK STUPID !

HEAD FOR EVEN MORE SUPER SOCCER ACTION!

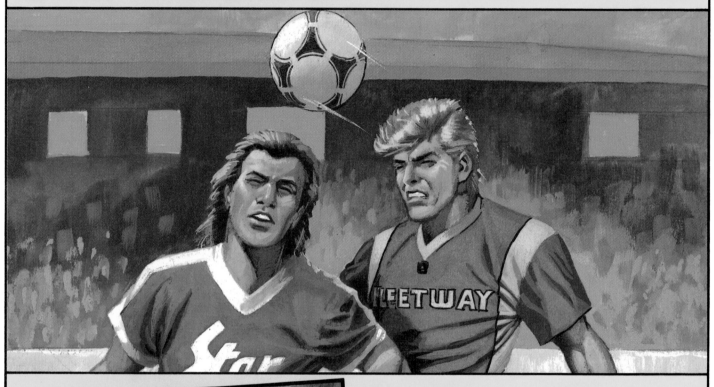

There's much more Melchester Magic in the Roy of the Rovers Colour Album Number One. Not one, not two, but SIX sensational soccer stories featuring Roy Race and the mighty men of Melchester. For every fan of football ... for every fan of Melchester Rovers Football Club, Roy's Colour Album Number One is a MUST!

IT'S A FABULOUS FEAST OF FOOTBALL!